ON LOVE'S PATH

New Versions *of*
Rumi, Kabir *&* Hafiz

ON LOVE'S PATH

New Versions *of* Rumi, Kabir & Hafiz

MARK RUSKIN

GREEN LOTUS PRESS
SANTA BARBARA, CALIFORNIA

ACKNOWLEDGEMENTS

Deep gratitude for my amazing family ~ Jan, Anya, Logan, and Melia
who give me a reason to live and love everyday.
Huge thanks and immense gratitude to Tricia and Stan Evenson of
Evenson Design Group for your remarkable friendship and unequaled
expertise in layout and design. You make beautiful books!
I want to acknowledge Jeroen Oosterhof for use of your extraordinary
photo "Lorien" for the front cover. You are a true artist of light!
Enormous thanks to Pamela Gray for your thorough editing, thoughtful
feedback, and kind encouragement. You inspire me to create!
Big appreciation to Jan Ruskin and Rochelle Teising for initial editing
with the early manuscript and for all your love and support.
Gratitude to Leslie Ekker, master of images, for your unique
eye and expertise in shooting the photo for the back cover.
Thank you to Elisabeth Donati for all your technical help.
Heartfelt gratitude to Adya for guiding me to remembrance and truth,
always reminding me to take the backwards step.
And to the One, of which we are all a part.

GREEN LOTUS PRESS
SANTA BARBARA, CALIFORNIA

ISBN 978-0-692-80985-3
Library Of Congress Control Number 2016919292

To the living spirits of Rumi, Kabir & Hafiz ~
and to Rochelle and Dan for the gift of life.

CONTENTS

KABIR

HAFIZ

INTRODUCTION

Rumi, the Twirling Sufi Mystic Lit By the Fire of Shams
Kabir, the Bengali Weaver of God's Sacred Warp and Holy Weft
Hafiz, the Illumined Persian Gardener of Wine and Light

———◦◦◦———

Like three winding rivers, each of these enlightened poets helps
guide us back home to the ocean of Oneness that is our source.
Their exquisite poetry is a constant invitation to witness the truths
that lie beneath the thick veils of our thoughts, perceptions, and
identities. Here, we are one and the same. Here, the experience of
unity consciousness is natural, and freedom our birthright. We are
repeatedly reminded that our essence is love, that the sacred resides
within, and that the world is not as it appears. Love is the common
denominator, and through it, the reality that we are not separate,
but are all one living spirit ~ each of us a unique manifestation and
expression of the One.

The message is clear: to open our hearts through the power of love
in order to see what is true. The directive is to look within and to
stop the incessant movement towards shiny objects and the world.
There is much pain to be found in the world, and much confusion
in the limits of a mind and a separate identity that needs something
from the world in order to feel whole, worthy, or complete. And so
we forget the deepest truths within us and mindlessly run towards
the things that hurt and disappoint in search of the one thing that
we actually possess.

I

This is the purpose of real teachers and good friends like these ~
to help point the way toward the sacred and timeless work of being
human. It's not an easy task, and remembrance is often followed by
deep forgetfulness activated by a lifetime of fear and conditioning.
This is why returning to the internal work, no matter where we are
on the path, is the key to liberation. As Rumi reminds us:

> Grapes take their time turning to wine,
> they must relax and ferment in the bottle.
> If you want your heart to open,
> you must feel life's fullness ~
> you must work at it;
> you must do the difficult work.

These poems are an open secret, a call to wake up to the sacred at
the root of our human experience. They remind us to always return
to love, to what is most true in us, and to surrender everything else.
They teach, support, and instruct like a trusted friend or a true
spiritual teacher. In their deep wisdom, clarity, and transcendent
beauty, they are timeless guideposts on this endless journey homeward.

*   *   *

I'm immensely grateful for these three profound guides and friends
for revealing themselves to me over the years. Without warning,
they each moved in and took up residence inside me, demanding
my attention in a most dynamic and unusual way. They cleared a
space for themselves and encouraged me on this journey, these new
versions ~ ancient wine in new skins. This is the mysterious work
of creation, of the heart that opens to truth and reveals something
new. So these versions are not intended to be scholarly, but rather

the offering of one who has been touched by the deep wellspring and expression of life and the opportunity to share the love anew.

I am indebted to the many translators of these three great mystic poets whose works I've used to create these new versions. For the gifts of Rumi, I am eternally in debt to A.J. Arberry and R.A. Nicholson whose dedication and prolific translations have seeded Rumi into full bloom. I am also grateful to Coleman Barks for his lifelong contributions in creating new versions of Rumi and reigniting the passion of this great Sufi mystic. It was his versions I first came across as a young man. For the gifts of Kabir, I am deeply indebted to Rabindranath Tagore whose *Gitanjali* has become a living truth inside my life. And for the gifts of Hafiz, I am especially grateful to H. Wilberforce Clarke whose immense *Divan-I-Hafiz* is a staggering accomplishment and a true jewel in the mud. Also, great thanks and deep admiration for the works of Gertrude Bell, Queen of the Desert, a truly remarkable woman.

Mark Ruskin
Santa Barbara, California
September 22, 2016

RUMI

A Quarry Filled with Gold

ONLY LOVE IN THE WORLD

Include yourself in life's community
if you want the bliss of an open heart.
Walk inside the tavern
if you want to be with the drunkards.
Empty the cup of passion
and you'll never feel ashamed.
Close your worldly eyes,
and you'll begin to see
with your inner eye.

Hold your arms wide open
if it's Love's embrace you're after.
Break open the clay image
if it's the face of reality you want to see.
Why, for the sake of a crone,
do you tolerate such a large dowry?

At night, the Beloved always comes to me ~
refrain from eating opium tonight;
don't open your mouth to food
and you will taste Love's sweetness.
Listen, the bearer of Love's cup
is no tyrant, and inside
lies a gathering of souls.

Come take your seat inside this circle ~
how long are you willing to stay separate?

Look, it's really quite a bargain!
Give up your one little life
and gain the entire universe!

Stop acting like dogs and wolves
and feel the inherent love of the shepherd.
You say, "But my enemy betrayed me!"
You must let it all go if you really want
to walk through Love's doorway.

Think of nothing,
only of the One who created thought.
Tending your soul is more essential
than caring for your daily bread.

When God's earth is so vast and spacious,
why have you fallen asleep inside a prison?
Your mind is a knot; untie it with silence
and the explanations of Eden.

Resist speaking, so you may
truly speak in the word to come.
Surrender your life and the world,
and you will witness only love in the world.

A QUARRY OF SWEET THINGS

My secret thoughts are the veiled treasures,
and I am the one who plunders them.

If I freely reveal the treasure,
then I am the one who is crazy!

The real lunatic is the one
who has not gone completely mad.
He has encountered the night guards,
but still wanders the streets.

My secret thoughts are vast,
they are no accident,
and this priceless jewel cannot
be obtained in the world.

I am a quarry of sweet things;
I am an endless field of sugar cane ~
they grow out of my body,
and at the same time,
I am consuming them.

LISTEN TO THE REED'S STORY

Listen to the reed's story of separation.
It sings, "Ever since I was cut from the reed-bed,
my suffering has caused everyone around me to weep."
I desire a heart broken open
with the pain of severance and heart-longing.
Everyone who is separated from their source
longs to return home.

Everywhere I go, I share my sorrowful story
and mingle with both the joyful
and the troubled ones.
Everyone becomes my friend,
but no one seeks out my inner secrets.
My secret is really my suffering,
but the senses can't begin to comprehend it.

The body isn't veiled from the soul,
nor the soul from the body ~
but the eyes can never see the soul.
So the reed's song is really
made of fire, not of air:
whoever is without this fire
cannot truly live.
It is Love's fire that plays the flute!
It is Love's passion that enters the wine!

The reed is a friend to all who have lost
something precious.
Its cry breaks open our hearts.
Have you ever seen such a poison
and an antidote like the reed?

Have you ever seen such a compassionate
and longing lover?
The reed sings the course of blood,
telling the story of Majnun's passion.
This sense is revealed only to the senseless.
The tongue has no other customer but the ear.

Inside the pain of our days, our hearts
burn with the fire of grief's longing.
If our days have passed, then let them go!
The past doesn't exist.
But who you are remains.
And nothing is as sacred as
the presence of you.

You must be a fish
to really appreciate Love's water,
or else be completely drowned.
Without your daily bread,
the day can seem very long.
The raw can't begin to understand
the condition of the ripe,
so my words will be brief:
Farewell!
Friend, break your chains
and be free!
Only you can do this!
How long will you be a slave
to shiny objects?

If you were to pour an ocean into a pitcher,
could it store more than one day's worth?
Your greedy eyes, like the pitcher,
can never be filled.
The oyster shell has no pearl
until it is satisfied.

Only the one whose clothes
are ripped by Love's hand,
is free of greed and all imperfections.
Greetings to the One who brings Love's gain,
the healer of all illness,
the cure for all our pride and arrogance.

Only with Love could these earthly bodies fly,
could the mountains ripple and begin to dance.
Love awoke Mount Sinai, my dear,
and made Sinai so drunk that Moses fainted!

If my lips were pressed against
the One who knew me well,
like the reed, I too would tell
everything that could be told.

But, separated from those who
speak my language, I became silent,
although a hundred songs sang inside me.

When the garden has wintered over,
and the rose has been pruned,
you won't hear the nightingale's song.

The Beloved is everything,
the lover only a veil ~
the Beloved is a living thing,
the lover already dead.
Without Love's arrival, the lover
is like a bird without wings.

How could I be conscious and aware
without the awareness of the Beloved?
Love desires that this world be shared.
If the mirror of your soul shows no reflection,
it's time to clean the rust that's accumulated there.

Friends! Listen closely to this story:
it is the truth and marrow
of what is most vital and alive inside.

A BEAUTIFUL BATHHOUSE

Humanity's being is a beautiful bathhouse,
wondrous and warm.

When you're in the bath,
you can never actually see
that the fire comes from *inside* you.

Inside lives the heat of the mind,
the heat of the spirit,
and the heat of the soul.
Only when you leave the bathhouse,
and move to the other world,
can you begin to grasp
the essence of each.

As long as you're in the bathhouse
you'll never actually see the fire,
only feel its mysterious effects.
It would be similar to throwing someone
who has never seen water
into the ocean,
blindfolded!

They feel something wet and soft
against their skin,
but they don't actually know what it is.
When the blindfold is removed,
they see that it is water.
Beyond mere impressions
lies the perception of its waterness.

IF YOU CALL ME

Therefore, ask of God
what is in your heart
without hesitation.
It will not be in vain.
God says, "If you call me,
I will hear you."

BY DIGGING DOWN DEEP

It's only natural for lover and Beloved
to be totally informal.
Formalities are for those who are separate.
Informality is not truly possible
without the presence of Love.

A lover can never prove his Beloved's beauty,
nor can anyone ever convince him of anything
that would ever cause even a hint of hatred.

Logical proofs don't work here!
Here, you must be a seeker
and a friend of the Beloved.

It's not time to speak
more words about this ~
but try with your whole being
to reach into the waters of your heart
by digging down deep.

IF YOU'RE REALLY LOVE'S LOVER

If you're really Love's lover,
you must never stop seeking Love!
Take a sharp blade
and cut the throat of shyness forever!

Your reputation and your name
only distract you on the path.
This is the truth ~
hear it with a clear mind
and be silent.

Don't ask why the lunatic works lunacy
in a million varied forms,
or why the crazy one continues
with his constant deceptions.

First he leases a cloak,
then scales a mountain;
now he's sipping poison,
and finally dances with death.

SPIRIT'S GOLD

You are the soul's homecoming
in this season of suffering.
You are Spirit's gold
in this pain of separation.
Everything my mind can't imagine,
everything beyond understanding
comes from you,
and points me towards you
in silent worship.

With your blessing, my loving gaze
stays focused on eternity.
Your abundance grants me great wealth.
Your concealed treasures open
all of Reality to me.

I kneel down to you with all of my heart and soul.
I lay my face in the dust of this Earth and proclaim:
There is such a Love as you for me!

Union occurs where life is eternal ~
time has no home here!
Life is the cauldron,
union is the elixir inside ~
without you, what good is the pain
of this vessel to me?

THE BEAUTY OF SHAMS

That drunken moon has returned,
the one the sky has never seen
except in its dreams,
and it's brought with it a fire
that even the ocean couldn't quench.

Made drunk and empty
by the cup of Love,
I see my soul and inhabit
the temple of my body.

The proprietor of this tavern
has become my Heart-Friend.
My blood has transformed to wine
and my heart to a sumptuous feast.

When my inner seeing is filled with Love,
the inner voice speaks:
Perfect, this vessel of fragrant wine!

In my house, where sunlight falls
in beams of rapture,
the fingers of Love pull up all the flowers
from the roots.

My heart suddenly saw the sea of Love
and leapt after the flooding tides, screaming
Discover me!

15

The beauty of Shams, the glory of Tabriz,
is the shining sun
in the path of heart's misting vapors
moving forever forward.

———◦∞◦———

LOVE'S DISCIPLE

Love's disciple is drunk without wine,
complete without food,
confused and astonished.

Love's disciple is sovereign
beneath the dervish's cloak,
needing no nourishment or sleep.

Love's disciple is a jewel
amid the wreckage,
untouched by fire and water.

Love's disciple is beyond
atmosphere and solid ground,
a sea without beginning or end.

Love's disciple offers
precious pearls
without any effort or time.

Love's disciple holds
thousands of Moons and Skies
in her infinite folds.

Love's disciple shines
with a hundred thousand
blazing Suns of light.

Love's disciple becomes wise
by living the truth,
needing no scriptures or books.

Love's disciple is free of betrayal and religion,
transcending all notions
of right and wrong.

Love's disciple is separate from
being and non-being,
surrounded by angels of constant blessing.

Love's disciple is veiled,
Shamsi-Din, light of the Sun,
the One we seek and meet at least!

———◦∞◦———

NEW TREASURE IS OURS

The voice of Love emanates
from everywhere and in all directions.
If you're headed for heaven,
why waste your time sightseeing?

New treasure is ours!
Now we're only concerned with soul-work.
Mustafa is the leader of our caravan,
majesty of the world!
The storm's honeyed scent emanates
from the lock of his curls.
This thought's radiance germinates
from the light of his cheek.

We all belong to heaven because
we're all friends of the angels.
So, let us return to that ecstasy, and
we'll fly even higher than heaven or angels,
passing beyond the sacred pair.

On this journey,
we're all headed for greatness
and transcendence!

A PRICELESS PEARL

Such a priceless pearl as you ~
who can name your worth?
All worthy things in this world
are ultimately a gift from you.

What could be worse than spending a life
not gazing at your face?

In the swell of life's ocean,
become Love's friend and escape
by swimming out of all calamity.

Nothing is permanent in this world,
so regard all things as perishable,
separate from your eternal nature.

How ecstatic the king
that is mated by your rook!
What perfect company we keep
when you are always present!

I can't stop placing myself at your feet,
O Shamsi Tabriz,
most beautiful and glorious of all sights!
This king is a beggar for you,
heart and soul!

THERE'S NO NEED TO SUFFER

All forms have their origin in the formless.
When the form dies, who do you grieve
if the source is eternal?
Every magnificent sight you have ever seen,
all the profound truths you have witnessed,
they're all still awake and alive *in* you.

There's no need to suffer!
Think of God as a fountain,
and all manifest things
as rivers flowing from
that eternally flowing fountain.
As long as there's a fountain,
there will always be flowing rivers.

Let go of your grief
and never stop gulping this river water!
This is the water that always quenches
and never, ever runs dry.

From the very beginning,
a ladder was placed in front of you
so that you had some possibility of escape.
From mineral, you changed to plant life,
and then to animal. It's no secret!
Eventually, you evolved to become human
with innate wisdom, reasoning,
and fidelity to truth.

Regard your body, which has grown
out of this Earth ~
How perfect and beautiful it has become!
After you've evolved from being human,
you will undoubtedly become an angel,
and then you'll have no more need of this Earth.
You are bound for heaven!
Then you'll move even beyond
the place of angels.

Dive into *that* ocean, where your single drop
becomes a thousand seas of Oman.
Move beyond daughter and son
and be the One with all of your soul.
When your body finally ages,
what does it really matter
if your soul is still young?

———◦∞◦———

LOVE ASKED

Love asked, "Who is at my door?"
I said, "Your devoted servant."
Love asked, "What is it that you want?"
I said, "To honor you."
Love asked, "How long will you advance?"
I said, "Until you summon me."
Love asked, "How long will you burn?"
I said, "Until I am consumed."
I committed myself to Love
and surrendered all control and authority.
Love said, "With commitment
comes the need of a witness."
I said, "Tears and longing are my witness."
Love asked, "What are your intentions?"
I said, "Perseverance and devotion."
Love asked, "What do you want from me?"
I said, "All your blessings."
Love asked, "Who do you keep company with?"
I said, "Only the thought of you, dear One."
Love asked, "What drew you here?"
I said, "The perfume of your cup."

EVERYTHING ELSE IS COUNTERFEIT

Anyone who doesn't wear
the robes of true Love
shames the fabric of existence.
Love is all there is,
so why not be drunk with it?

Without mingling with true Love,
there really is no way to the Beloved.
When they ask, "What is Love?"
just say, "Surrendering the will."
If you haven't yet escaped from will,
you're still a prisoner of it.

Enfold the soul
which is enfolded by nothing.
How long are you willing to dance
with a dead lover?

The real lover is sovereign,
guiding over the two worlds
in form and the formless.
It is only Love and the lover
that live eternally.
So set your mind only on Love ~
everything else is counterfeit.

Always be open to wonder!
My dear, there is no greater death
than constant expectation.

IT'S ONLY YOUR IMAGINATION

The garden is confused and can't tell
the difference between leaf and blossom.
The birds are absent-minded
and don't know which is the trap,
and which the bait.

This is the One Love of heaven
mirroring Venus and the Moon,
whose house has no boundaries and no end.

There is no separation or injury here,
only Love and grace.
It's only your imagination
that sees bars on the door.

So set fire to your life and stay silent!
Retract your tongue ~ have you ever noticed
how often it brings you only harm?

KINDLED LIGHT

The sweet fragrance of the Beloved
continually emanates
from the deepest center of my soul.
Why would I ever stray
from the core of Love's heart?

Last night I walked into Love's garden
with a desire to merge.
The Beloved's Sun shone through my eyes
and a stream of tears began to flow.
Every ecstatic rose that sprouts
from Love's laughing lips
had avoided the thorns of existence,
had escaped Ali's great sword.
Every leaf and blade of grass was swaying
and dancing madly in the fields
though the unknowing would only see them
as immobile and still.
And then suddenly the cypress revealed itself
so that the whole garden became drunk
and the horizon arose and clapped its hands!

In this divine orchard of union,
there's no room for numbers,
although numbers exist in the world
of the five senses and the four elements.

You can number a hundred thousand
sweet apples inside your hands,
but if you really want to come to One,
crush them all together!

You are Love's fire:
your face is a flame,
your wine, kindled light.
The soul merges with each and asks,
Really, where is there to go?

Speak heart's language
without using words.
The purity of a clear heart is born
from constant soul activity.

Shamsi Tabriz is the sun seated
on a sparkling, jeweled throne,
and my poems are arranged around him
like so many surrendered servants.

———◦∞◦———

A MERCHANT OF LOVING GLANCES

Since you've opened up your house
as a merchant of loving glances,
disperse them the way light does ~
with silent, closed lips.

I make no complaints but
keep my distance
from the unknowing.
You are all that is worthy in this life,
yet the mystery of you
remains veiled.

Come now,
like the rising Sun of Tabriz
blazing in the East ~
behold the triumphant star
and the victory banner waving
in the morning wind!

A QUARRY FILLED WITH GOLD

Although you possess no legs,
choose to travel *inside* yourself.
There is a mine of rubies waiting there,
engraved with splintered sunlight.

Make this pilgrimage out of yourself,
into yourself.
This journey will reveal that you are
a quarry filled with gold.

Move from pain and sorrow into joy.
From this salty Earth, a thousand
kinds of fruits may ripen.

From the Sun, the glory of Tabriz,
recognize the miracles all around you
like the brilliance of a tree
growing into the light
of such a beauty as this.

FROM THE POCKET OF MY HEART

I choose you alone in this world.
Will you let me continue to suffer?

My heart is a pen in your hands,
composing all these changing moods,
from brightest joy to darkest sorrow.

I surrender my will to you ~
what can I actually see
other than what you show me?

You are the gardener in me who grows
both the thorn and the rose.
Sometimes I smell the roses and
sometimes I pull out the thorns.

If you enjoy me as *that*, I am *that*.
If you prefer me as *this*, I am *this*.
Who am I, inside this vessel,
where you give constant, changing
color to my soul?

You are the first, and you will be the last ~
When you're hidden from me,
I am one of the infidels.
When you're here with me,
I am one of the faithful.

I am nothing
but what you have made of me.
What do you seek
from the pocket of my heart?

———◦∞◦———

I'M NOT OF THIS WORLD

I don't recognize myself anymore!
I'm neither Christian nor Jew;
not Zoroastrian, nor Muslim.
I'm not of the East, and
I'm not of the West.
I'm not of the land, nor of the sea.

I'm not of Earth's design,
nor am I a billion spinning galaxies.
I'm not of Earth, Air, Fire, or Water.
I'm not of the Cosmos, nor of the dust.
I'm not of existence, nor of being.

I'm not of India, nor of China,
not of Saqsin, nor of the Bulgars.
I'm not of the land of Iraq,
nor of the region of Khorasan.

I'm not of this world, nor of the next,
not of Heaven, nor of hell.
I'm not of Adam, nor of Eve,
not of Eden, nor of Rizwan.

My place is of no-place,
my trace is of no-trace.
I'm not of the body, nor of the soul.
I exist only in the heart of my Beloved.

I have done away with duality
and have witnessed the two worlds
and seen them as one!
O Shamsi Tabriz,
I'm so drunk in this world
that except for this
wild rapture and ecstasy,
I have no story to tell!

WANTING WHAT IS REAL

You, who are milk and honey.
You, who are Sun and Moon.
You, who are mother and father.
I've known no real family but you.

Immortal Love, divine minstrel ~
you are both the waiting and the refuge.
I've found none equal to you.

There is steel in our hearts,
but your love acts as a magnet.
You are the true source of
wanting what is real ~
all aspirations come from you alone.

Silence friend!
Put knowledge and the world
behind you.
Until you spoke of the world,
I knew none but you.

SUCH PROFOUND OPENING

Listen! This is love:
to forever fly up to heaven ~
to tear, every moment,
a hundred veils ~
from the first,
to renounce the world ~
the final step,
to walk without feet ~
to view this world as invisible
and finally let go of all appearances.

O my heart of hearts, I said,
may it bless you to enter
the circle of lovers,
to see beyond what your
mortal eyes see,
to penetrate the labyrinth
of the heart.

When did this breath
first come to you, my soul?
When did my heart experience
such profound opening?

JUST THE TWO OF US

Unspeakable joy when
we're together in Love's palace,
just the two of us.

We fill two shapes, but share one soul,
just the two of us.

The radiance of illuminated gardens
and the melody of birdsong
will surely bring us immortality,
as we enter the grove of eternity,
just the two of us.

The Stars and Planets
will turn their gaze to us,
and we'll show them the Moon's glory,
just the two of us.

Separated no more,
we mingle in the ecstasy of union,
blissfully free from idle talk,
just the two of us.

Every peacock in heaven is consumed
with envy
when they hear our laughter together,
just the two of us.

And wonder of all wonders
that the two of us,
sitting here together in the same alcove,
are also at this very moment
in both Iraq and Khorasan!

————⸺◁∞▷⸺————

TAKE YOUR ONE SEAT

When Love's illustrious presence says *Fly*,
why doesn't the soul immediately take wing?

And how can a fish flopping on the shore
not leap towards the water when it hears
the lapping waves of Love's ocean?

And why shouldn't the falcon flee
from the quarry, back to the King,
when it hears the drum-beat of *Return*?

And why shouldn't every Sufi begin dancing
like a drunken dust mote, in the sunlight of eternity,
to finally witness Reality in the spinning?

There is so much astounding
beauty and grace here,
where the waters of life forever flow.
It would be a grave error
not to jump into these waters!

Fly, bird of the soul,
back to the land of your origins.
You've finally escaped your cage ~
your wings are spread wide!
Fly away from life's cruel rivers
towards the wide open oceans inside.

Leave the doorway, my friend,
and take your one seat
on the throne of your life.

ONE KIND OF LOVE

The human being is one kind of love,
made of pain, desire, and craving ~
and even if one possesses
a hundred thousand pleasures,
there's still no peace or calm inside.

People are drawn to their own unique
preferences and inclinations
but find no ultimate fulfillment in them
because what they're really wanting
can't be found there.
Only the Beloved can saturate the heart
with real peace.
How can peace be found anywhere else?

Everything in the world
is like a ladder ~
you push off one rung and climb to the next.
To stop on one rung is to suffer.
The quicker we can awaken and see Reality,
the shorter the path,
and the less we waste time in life
clinging to each unstable rung.

A HUNTING EXPEDITION

There was once a Lion who brought with him
a wolf and a fox on a hunting expedition.
They were quickly able to catch and kill
a wild ox, an ibex, and a hare.

The Lion ordered the wolf
to divide the food between them.
The wolf suggested that the Lion enjoy the ox,
he would feast on the ibex,
and the fox would make do with the hare.

The Lion became furious, roaring
"You presume to speak of 'I' and 'you'
and 'my portion' and 'your portion'
when it's all the Lion's!"

With one quick swipe of his paw,
he killed the wolf and turned to the fox.
"You divide the food," he said.
The fox, humbled by what he had witnessed,
proclaimed, "But it is all yours!"

The Lion was happy with the fox's self-denial
and told him, "You are no longer a fox
but my very own Self."

NOT ENOUGH SPACE

Once, a friend of the Beloved
knocked on her Friend's door.
The Beloved asked, "Who are you?"
"It is me," she answered.

Her Beloved Friend said,
"You are forbidden entrance here.
There's no place for the raw
at my well-done banquet table.
Nothing but the pain of separation
can cook the one who is raw
and free her of all pretense.
Since you still indulge in your self,
you must feel the fiery pain of longing."

The dejected woman journeyed
inside herself for an entire year,
burning with despair and separation.
Finally, her heart was fully cooked,
and so she approached
her Beloved Friend's house once again.
She knocked on the door
with a certain amount of apprehension,
afraid something displeasing
would slip from her mouth.

Her Beloved Friend inquired,
"Who is that at my door?"
She answered, "It is you who is at the door,
my One Beloved."
"Since it's me, then let me enter,
for there's not enough space for two
in this one house."

———⊷∞⊷———

A DEEP SLEEP FELL UPON YOU

Lovers! Lovers!
It's time to leave this world behind!
My inner ear hears the beat of the drums
that announces our departure.
Look! The camel driver readies his row of camels ~
he begs to be forgiven.
Why is everyone in this caravan still asleep?

The sound you hear is the great hum
of departure and camel bells.
Every moment another soul is slipping out
into the great unknown.
From the blue-dome of the heavens
comes the true soul of the One
whose mysteries may be revealed at last.

A deep sleep fell upon you
while you were out circling the universe ~
for the sake of this light-filled life,
beware this sleep that is so heavy!
Friend, seek the Beloved!
Watchman, be ever wakeful!
It would serve a sentry to stay awake!

THE CRY OF RETURN

I went to Love's home and asked.
"Where is the Beloved?"
"The Beloved is wandering from town to town
drunk and in love," they told me.

"I'm obliged to follow," I said.
"I'm Love's friend
and have no enemies in this world.
Can you give me any guidance?" I asked.

"The Beloved has fallen in love
with the Gardner," they said.
"Go look in gardens and along riverbeds."

All delirious lovers seek the object
of their true love ~
A fish that's only known water
never looks for dry land.

How does a lover remain inside such
brilliant waves of perfume and color?

Piles of fresh snow melt into flowing water
once they've looked into the eyes of the Sun.
Copper turns to gold once it is touched
and hears the cry of *Return*.

YOU CAN MINE A WEALTH OF RUBIES

Come now, don't wait!
You'll never find a companion
that quenches quite like me.
Where do you expect
to find a Beloved such as me
anywhere in this world?

Come now, and stop wasting your time
walking back and forth in a straight line.
Your currency has no value
in any other marketplace.

You're a dry riverbed
and I am heavy rains.
You're a destroyed city
and I am the Master Builder.

Joy comes through me
like a flash of light, or not at all.
In your dreams there are a thousand
shifting forms, but when your dream is over,
they all scatter and disappear.

Close your eyes that see falsely
and open the eye that sees clearly.
Your senses are like a donkey,
and human desire is the bridle.

Follow the sweet nectar
that flows through the garden of Love,
for life can be a seller of sour vinegar
and a vintner of unripened grapes.

Travel the path to Love's hospital.
You don't want to forsake
a healer such as me!
Without my royalty, this world
resembles a body without a head.
Wrap yourself like a turban
around such a head!

Until you empty yourself completely,
hold on to the mirror ~
the soul is your real reflection,
the body only rust.

Where can you find the Master Merchant
and eagerly barter
to acquire such priceless gold?

Never cease thinking of me, the One
who gave you the gift of thought.
From my body, you can mine
a wealth of rubies.

Come now, run towards me,
the One who provided you with feet!
Look at me with your blessed eyes,
the One who provided you with sight!

Let us clap our hands together
and stir up Love's sea-foam,
for our joy has no room
for pain or victimhood.

Listen to me without your ears!
Speak to me without your tongue!
The speech of the tongue can cause
so much confusion and harm.

WHEN LOVE'S ROBES ARE LOOSENED

Although this Earth is a slave to the Sky,
and the body to the spirit,
what does the Earth actually give up
in this sacred encounter?
What benevolence did reason
ever contribute to the body?

It doesn't serve you to hide under a rug
beating your drum all alone.
Find your courage and plant your flag
in the desert sand.

Listen closely with your spirit-ears:
from the green arch of the sky
the passionate cry of lovers
comes drifting in.

When Love's robes are loosened
by the quickening of longing,
witness ecstasy's victory,
and Orion's confusion.

The world, so full of
better and *worse*,
has no room for Love,
which transcends all notions
of *better* and *worse*.

When the Sun rises, where does the night go?
When the heart opens,
where is there any room for pain or separation?
Be silent awhile and listen.

Speak now, O Soul of souls,
from the desire of whose face
every single thing became articulate.

LIT BY YOUR MOONLIKE FACE

Tonight, all of space celebrates union
with talk of a coming bride ~
the full Moon from a scattered sky.

Venus is beside herself
listening to such beautiful tunes,
like the nightingale who becomes drunk
with Spring's budding rose.

Watch the North Star in its admiration of Leo,
and see the stardust that Pisces
is whipping up from afar!

Jupiter gallops on his horse
towards his old friend Saturn, calling
*Reclaim your youth~ go now
and bring good news back to us!*

While the bloodied hand of Mars,
clutching his sword, has changed into
a life affirming Sun,
spreading good deeds all across creation.

Aquarius has become drenched
with the waters of life
and rains down liquid pearls
upon the dried-out body of Virgo.

The Pleiades have expanded
and become so generous
that they no longer fear Libra ~
and why should Aries retreat or
ever be afraid of Hera?
The heart of Sagittarius
has been pierced
by the glance of the Moon,
and he swoons in passion for her,
much like Scorpio.

With such a festival of union as this,
go and surrender Taurus,
or else you may end up walking
drunk in the mud-like Cancer.

The sky is a starry dome
and the only reality is Love ~
whatever can be said of Love,
always look deeper to the true meaning.

Shams-I-Tabriz,
through your illuminated dawn,
darkness of night turns to bright day,
lit by your Moonlike face.

HAPPINESS RIGHT NOW

The time has come!
Today is a day for celebration!
From now on, joy and fulfillment
grow and expand.
Clap your hands and proclaim,
There is happiness right now!
From the very beginning,
this day was blessed
and made manifest in perfection.

There is no other in this world
anything like our Friend!
No one has witnessed such a day as this
in over a hundred ages!
All of Earth and space are filled
with the Friend's sweetness ~
everywhere you look,
sugarcane is sprouting!

The blast of the scattering seas arrive,
and the land is filled with waves
from those invisible waters.

Any coin not minted here is counterfeit ~
any wine not pressed
from the cup of the soul remains separate.

SUCH A BEAUTY AS THIS

I see a Moon outside the eye
in the eye,
which the eye has not seen,
nor the ear heard.

I can't see tongue, heart,
or soul outside myself
since I first glimpsed that lovely cheek.

If Plato hadn't caught sight
of that most beautiful Moon,
he would have ended up
even crazier than I am!

In the mirror of eternity,
time is reflected.
In the mirror of time,
before-eternity can be seen.
Inside this mirror,
the two are woven together
in the Beloved's braids.

From clouds outside the senses
come rains of pure spirit
washing the dust of the body ~
what an exalted downpour!

The beautiful Moon-Faced One
saw Love's reflection and became humbled
by such a beauty as this.

SOMETHING MORE CRUCIAL

Listen! Which is sweeter:
sugar, or the hidden One
who makes sugar?
Which is more lovely:
the Moon, or the One
who made the Moon?

Let go of sugar!
Surrender the Moon!
There is something
more crucial behind both:
look for that!

Under the ocean waves lie
colorful pearls and endless treasures,
but nothing close to the Beautiful One
who made the ocean and the pearls.

There are other waters flowing,
arising from an endless waterwheel
which feeds the heart in its perfect turning.

You can't create an image of a bathhouse
without knowledge of what a bathhouse is.
Can you imagine the knowledge
that created consciousness and intelligence?

MAY THIS MARRIAGE

May this wedding and this marriage
be forever blessed.

May it always be sweet and full,
like milk and honey
this marriage, like wine and halvah.

May this marriage provide
shade and abundant fruit,
like the royal date palm.

May this marriage overflow with laughter,
and always open into paradise.

May this marriage be filled
with compassion and real happiness,
now and in the years ahead.

May this marriage grow deep roots,
ground in integrity,
and reach for the Moon
in the ever-wakeful blue sky.

There are no more words
to express how Spirit mingles
inside this marriage.

GOD'S TREASURED ONES

You'll never see reason go the way of despair.
Love, on the other hand,
will run towards it with open arms.
Love is reckless, but never reason.
Reason seeks only gain.

The lover is burning, unabashed,
coming on suddenly with a racing heart.
Though with sorrow, Love is a millstone
grinding us down to the truth,
free of any self interest.

Love gambles everything and seeks nothing,
with no concern for gain or reward.
Love receives everything as a pure gift from God.

Existence without cause,
the lover offers life up again and again,
without cause.
Such is devotion: a giving up of one's self
which transcends all religion.

Religion favors grace and devotion,
but those who gamble everything away,
and all at once, are God's treasured ones ~
they don't put God to the test,
nor do they knock on the door of gain or loss.

THIS HUMAN BODY IS A GUESTHOUSE

This human body is a guesthouse ~
each morning a new guest comes running in.
Try not to say, "This guest is such a burden,"
or she'll fly back into nothingness.

Like a guest, all your thoughts and feelings
come to you from the other world.
Entertain them all!
Whether friend or thief,
they are all a gift on the path.

Every day, every moment,
thoughts enter your heart like honored guests.
Dear soul, regard each one as you would a person,
as each person's worth is rooted
in thought and spirit.

If heartache fills your thoughts,
it's only getting you ready
for the joy that's to follow.
It forcefully sweeps your house clean,
making room for the new joy to enter in
from the source of all goodness.

It scatters the falling leaves
from the branches of the heart,
so new green leaves may sprout.
It overturns the old joy so new joys may manifest
from the source of all that exists.

Sorrow can help pull up the rotten roots,
revealing the true Source that is veiled from sight.
Whatever sorrow causes the heart
to finally surrender and release,
invites in something far better in exchange ~
especially to the one who intuitively knows
that sorrow is the aid of the intuitives.

Unless there are dark clouds and lightning,
the smiling Sun will burn the vines.
Good fortune, bad fortune,
let both be welcomed guests in your heart.

Like transiting planets,
they move from sign to sign.
When a favorable or unfavorable planet
moves into your house, adapt yourself to it.
Be as congenial as possible,
so when it reunites with the Moon,
it will speak of you with gratitude
to the Lord of the Heart.

THIS GAME OF DEVOTION

In the Beloved's home,
where are *We* and *I*?
That One, free from *We* and *I*:
the fragrant essence of all life!

When man and woman join as one,
you are that One ~
where individuality is annihilated,
you are that union.

Did you create this *We* and *I*
so you could play this game of devotion
with yourself? ~
so all *I*'s and *you*'s should dissolve
into One Soul,
and at last be drowned inside you?

Every dawn shines in the East
with abundant grace,
blessed by the Sun's radiant face.
How was it that you evaded
your delirious lover,
you with your sweet lips
beyond measure or worth?

Wine becomes drunk with us,
not we with it ~
the body came into being from us,
not we from the body.

We are like the bees,
our bodies the honeycomb ~
we have made the body, like wax,
slowly over time, bit by bit.

THE DIFFICULT WORK

David spoke, "My Beloved,
since you have no real need of us,
what benefit was there in creating
the two worlds of form and the formless?"

The Beloved spoke to him,
"O man in time, I was a concealed jewel
and desired that my treasures of love and abundance
should be revealed, so I created a mirror:
its front-side the spiritual heart,
its back-side the world."

If you don't know the face intimately,
the back will always seem better.

When clay and straw are mixed together,
how can you ever see anything there?
When clay and straw are separated,
the mirror becomes naturally clear.

Grapes take their time turning to wine,
they must relax and ferment in the bottle.
If you want your heart to open,
you must feel life's fullness ~
you must work at it;
you must do the difficult work.

KABIR

An Ecstatic Dance

I'M RIGHT BESIDE YOU

Friend, why are you searching for me?
Look, I'm right beside you.

I'm not in the temple or the mosque.
I'm not in the Kaaba or on Mount Kailash.
I'm not in rituals or traditions,
or in yoga or self-denial.

If you're a true seeker, you'll see me instantly.
You'll meet me in this timeless moment.
Kabir says, "O Holy One,
God is the breath within the breath."

THE BEAUTY THAT IS YOU

Don't go outside to the garden of flowers ~
Friend, don't go there!
Inside you there is a vast valley of flowers!
Take your seat on the thousand-petalled
lotus of the heart,
and behold the beauty that is you,
and everywhere.

WHILE YOU'RE STILL ALIVE

Friend, hope for the Beloved
while you're still alive.
Know the Beloved
while you're still living.
Understand now, for in this very life
liberation already lives.

If your bonds aren't severed
while you're alive,
what hope is there to be delivered
suddenly at death?

It's just an empty dream
that the soul will have union with God
because the body has passed.
If the Beloved is found now,
the Beloved will be found then.
If not, all that's left for us is an
empty room in the city of death.

If there's union now, there'll be union then.
So bathe in the truth of your being,
touch the true teacher inside,
and have deep faith in Reality.

Kabir says, "It's the longing for God
on the long search home that guides us ~
I'm a slave of this longing."

IT WANDERS OUTSIDE

The Moon shines inside of me,
but I'm blind and can't see it.
The Moon lives within,
and the Sun.

The silent drum of eternity
is playing within me,
but I'm deaf and can't hear it.

As long as we attach to the *I* and the *mine*,
our work in the world is meaningless.
When all attachment to the *I* and the *mine*
is gone, then God's work is done.

All work aims towards knowledge ~
when knowledge comes,
the work is complete.

The flower blooms in service of the fruit ~
when the fruit matures, the flower dies.
And although the musk is inside the deer,
it doesn't look within ~
it wanders outside in search of grass.

INSIDE THIS HUMAN VESSEL

Inside this human vessel lives
vast orchards and forest groves,
and the One who made
vast orchards and forest groves.

Inside this vessel are the seven oceans
and billions of spinning stars.

Inside is the touchstone
and the One who knows gold.

Within this vessel vibrates
the eternal sound,
where the bottomless well of sweet water
rises up forever.

Kabir says, "Listen my friend!
My Beloved lives inside of me!"

LOVE'S DIVINE REMEMBRANCE

My Beloved stays hidden and then,
in a flash of light, is revealed.

My Beloved crowns me with life
and removes all limitations.

My Beloved speaks
words of sorrow and words of joy,
but is the healing inside both.

I offer my body and mind to my Beloved ~
I surrender my entire life
to Love's divine remembrance.

I WAS DROWNING

You've drawn yourself close to me, my Love.
I was sleeping all alone and you woke me up,
singing to me with your sweet voice.

I was drowning in the ocean of this world,
and you came and saved me,
holding me tight in your arms.

Just one word without a second,
and you've allowed me to break
all my desires and attachments.
Kabir says, "Our hearts are now one."

IT'S THE SAME WATER

The ocean and the waves are one thing:
can you find any difference between
the ocean and the waves?
When the wave rises up, it's water,
and when it fall back, it's the same water.
Is there any difference between the two?

Just because we call it *wave*
doesn't mean that it's no longer water.

Inside God's body, the stars and galaxies
are stretched like beads being told.
Look at that string of beads with the eyes
of clear understanding.

KABIR CAUGHT A GLIMPSE

Between the conscious and the unconscious
the mind has woven a swing ~
on this swing hangs all of life,
and it never stops swaying,
back and forth and back and forth.

Billions of beings hang there,
with the Sun and the Moon
moving on their perfect courses.
Millions of ages pass,
and the swing sways on and on.

Everything in the universe is swinging:
the Cosmos, the Earth, the Air, the Water,
and the Beloved endlessly taking form.

Kabir caught a glimpse of this
and instantly became
a devoted servant.

YOU'VE BEEN ASLEEP

The Beautiful One is arriving!
Please wake up and run
to the foot of your Beloved.

The Beautiful One is standing
just next to your crown.

You've been asleep
for countless centuries ~
this morning,
won't you please wake up?

TRY NOT TO WANDER AWAY

To what distant shore are you
planning to cross?
There are no other travelers there,
and no road to travel by ~
do you see anyone walking or resting
on that so-called distant shore?

There's no river, no boat, and no boatman.
There's no towline
or anyone there to pull it
even if there were!

There's no Earth, no Sky, no time ~
nothing is actually there:
no shore and nothing to ford.

There is nobody there and no mind ~
do you think there's actually a place
that will finally quench
the soul's thirst?

You'll find absolutely nothing
in that emptiness.
So be strong and gain access
to your own body-temple,
for there you are firmly rooted.

Look deeply into this truth and try
not to wander away.
Kabir says, "empty yourself of all fantasies,
and stand solid in that which you are."

A REAL TEACHER

Friend, my heart longs for a real teacher,
the one who can fill Love's cup
and drink from it at will ~
the one who can offer it to me.

This is the teacher who can remove
the veil from my eyes, and finally show me
the face of my Beloved.
This is the teacher who can reveal
the whole universe, and play for me
the silent music of eternity.

This is the one who reveals that
joy and sorrow are one thing,
and always speaks the language of Love.

Kabir says, "The one with such a teacher
to guide one to sanity and safety,
has nothing left to fear."

IT'S THIS LONGING

I'm troubled day and night
and can't sleep.
It's this longing to merge with my Beloved.

The house of this world no longer
brings me any pleasure.

And then, an opening
in the sky of Being is revealed,
and the inner temple is seen.

I abandon my body and mind
at the foot of my Beloved.

OPEN THE WINDOW TO THE WEST

Night's thick shadows quickly gather
as Love's darkness wraps the body and mind.
Open the window to the West
and lose yourself in twilight's love.

Drink from the sweet nectar that saturates
the blooming lotus in your heart.
Ride the waves inside your body ~
there's so much radiance inside that ocean!

Listen! The music of conch shells,
the ringing of bells!
Kabir says, "Friend, know this:
the Holy One lives inside of me!"

THE DEVOTED LOVER

Love's path is a subtle conversation.
There's no asking, and no not-asking here,
only a falling down at Love's feet,
surrendered and lost in joy's longing ~
immersed in the depths of Love
like a fish at the bottom of the ocean.

The lover never hesitates to offer
their own head in service to Love.
Kabir says, "This is the true secret
of the devoted lover."

EXISTENCE IS AN ECSTATIC DANCE

All things come into being
through the sound of Om ~
the sacred vibration that animates
the love-body of form.

I am forever moving towards
union with you,
the One without a second:
timeless, formless, deathless,
everywhere, always.

That formless One takes on a billion forms:
Love made manifest in the world ~
yet pure and indestructible, it remains
infinite and beyond understanding.

Existence is an ecstatic dance
from which form rises up in waves.
When the wave comprehends that it's water,
body and mind dissolve,
and all that remains is joy.

The formless One is the source
of all consciousness,
eternal and beyond all joy and sorrow.
It is the kernel growing
within Spirit's bliss.

WHERE THAT BIRD IS RESTING

Perched in the tree of existence,
a bird dances with the ecstasy of life's joy.
No one knows where it first came from,
or the true meaning of its song.

In the shadow of the tree's branches,
the bird makes its nest,
coming in the evening
and leaving in the morning,
silent of its story and origin.

Why hasn't anyone told me about this bird
that has been singing inside me
for so very long?

It's neither colored nor colorless,
possessing no actual form or outline.
It simply sits in Love's shadow.

It lives beyond attaining or possessing,
infinite and eternal,
with no coming and no going.

Kabir says, "My friend,
the mystery of life is deep.
Let us seek the source and know
where that bird is resting."

WE ARE ONE AND THE SAME

When the heart is drunk with Love,
there's no need for words.

The precious diamond lives inside ~
there's no need to keep uncovering it
to make sure it's still sparkling.

When the load was light,
life's scale naturally went up ~
so now that it's full and complete,
there's really no need for weighing!

The swan has already departed to the ocean
beyond the mountains ~
the search in lakes and ponds
is no longer necessary.

The Beloved lives inside you ~
there's no need to search outside
with your earthly eyes.

Kabir says, "Listen friend!
My Beloved has made me blind with Love ~
we are one and the same!"

PENETRATED BY THE ARROW

My friend, wake up from your deep sleep.
The night has already passed ~
do you want to lose your days as well?

Others who have already woken up
have been rewarded with smiling jewels.

You're foolish to have wasted your time asleep!
Your lover, on the other hand, is wise.

You never took the time to prepare
your Beloved's bed,
but spent your time in fantasy and play.

Your entire youth was passed in vain
because you didn't recognize your Beloved.

Wake up! See! Your bed is empty.
Your lover left you in the night.
Kabir says, "You can only really wake up
if your heart is penetrated by the arrow
of Love's divine music."

LOVE'S KEY

The lock of false-seeing
closes the gate of being ~
open it with Love's key!

By opening this door,
you will wake up
the Beloved inside.

Kabir says, "Don't
pass this great treasure by!"

THE ONE WHO HAS CREATED EVERYTHING

Seeker, purify your body by the simple act of seeing.
Just as the seed lives within the banyan tree,
and within the seed lives the flowers,
the fruit, and the shade,
so the embryo lives within the body,
and within that embryo lives the body once again.

Fire, Air, Earth, Water, and Space ~
without the Beloved, none of these are possible.
Consider this, what really exists separate from the soul?
A pitcher full of water is put into more water ~
there's water inside and there's water outside.
Let's not give it a name,
or we'll confuse *Self* with *Other*.

Kabir says, "You must listen to what's true
at the core of your being.
Here, the Beloved speaks inside of you ~
the One who has created everything."

THE FISH IN THE OCEAN IS THIRSTY

I have to laugh when I hear
that the fish in the ocean is thirsty!

You don't see that what you really are
lives inside your own being,
and so you wander
from one forest temple to another
looking dazed and confused.

Kabir will tell you the truth:
it doesn't matter where you go,
to Varanasi or to Mathura ~
if you don't know your own soul,
the world will remain an illusion to you.

NO LIMITS OR BOUNDARIES

Who are you and where do you come from?
Where do you abide, and how is it that you have
your eternal play in this created world of yours?

The fire lives inside the wood,
but who is it that sparks it so suddenly?
And when the fire turns to ash,
where has the heat of the fire fled?

The true teacher shows
that there are no limits or boundaries.

Kabir says, "The Divine speaks
only the language that the listener
is capable of understanding."

A SECRET FLAG WAVES

A secret flag waves in the temple of the sky.
A blue dome hangs there, holding the Moon,
embedded with starry jewels.
Sunlight and Moonlight shine there ~
the place your mind finally stops,
silently adoring.

Kabir says, "Whoever drinks
from this nectar wanders the world
drunk and out of their mind."

THE INFINITE FLUTE

The infinite flute plays without end,
and its melody is always Love.
When Love arrives without limits,
then truth has been reached.
How far that soul-fragrance spreads
with no boundaries and no end!
Love's melody shines with the intensity
of a billion suns ~
without equal, the infinite flute
plays only notes of truth.

DEATH BECOMES UNREAL

What you see isn't real,
and what is real can't be named.
Until you actually see what is real,
you'll never truly believe or accept anything.

The person who actually knows
goes beyond words, and leaves
the ignorant standing in awe.

Whether you meditate on form or the formless,
only the one who sees knows
the Beloved beyond either.

Such beauty is beyond seeing!
Such music is beyond hearing!

Kabir says, "When you have found
true life in both Love and surrender,
then death becomes unreal to you."

ANY LASTING FULFILLMENT

When my Beloved is away,
my heart knows only pain ~
I feel dark in the daytime,
and my nights are empty and restless.
Who will listen to my sorrowful story?

The night can feel so black and empty,
and the hours pass by so slowly.
When my Beloved is away,
I suddenly arise in a panic,
shaking with fear.

Kabir says, "Listen my friend!
Only a date with the Beloved
will bring you any lasting fulfillment."

HEADED FOR DEATH'S DOOR

The seeker often dyes his robes
in the color-vat of the world ~
better he should dye his mind
in the cauldron of Love.

He prays inside an old, dark temple
while God is outside praising the Earth.

He pierces his ears with endless holes
and grows a tangled and matted beard
so that he resembles a goat.

He retreats to the wilderness,
attempting to extinguish
all his worldly and sexual desires.

He shaves his head
and regularly dyes his robes ~
he reads the Bhagavad-Gita
and can't stop talking
as if he knows something.

Kabir says, "As a matter of fact,
you're headed for Death's door
bound hand and foot!"

A POISED DAGGER

I don't know what kind of God
you've been imagining.
The seeker cries out loudly
to the Sacred One, but why?

Do you think that God is deaf?
The Sacred One can hear
even the quietest ring that the delicate
anklets of an insect make
as it walks across the garden.

Go and tell your beads,
mark your forehead with bright colors,
wear your long, matted locks
to appear a certain way ~
but if there's a poised dagger
inside your heart,
how will you ever really know God?

THE JEWEL THAT'S LOST IN THE MUD

Everyone's looking for the jewel that's lost in the mud.
Some look in the East, some look in the West.
Some look in the water, and others among stones.
But the servant Kabir knows its true value
and has wrapped it lovingly
in the lotus petals
of his heart.

YOUR VERY OWN HOMELAND

Open your eyes to Love,
and you'll see Love everywhere.

Look deeply into this truth,
and know that the entire world
is your very own homeland.

When you make contact with the true teacher,
your heart will naturally open.

Your teacher will reveal the secrets of Love
and non-attachment, and you will see that Love
transcends the entire universe.

IT LIVES IN SPRING'S PROMISE

I hear the infectious melody
that pours from Love's flute
and can't contain myself.

Although it's still winter,
the flowers are all in bloom,
and the bees have already received
their sacred invitation.

The sky thunders, lightning flashes,
and waves rise up inside my heart.
The rain is unceasing, and I long
for Love's sweet embrace.

Earth's rhythms rise and fall,
and there my heart finds its home ~
there the hidden flags are
whipping in the wind.

Kabir says, "Although my heart is dying,
it lives in Spring's promise."

MADE COMPLETELY OF LIGHT

The Holy Ones say that the unconditioned
stands behind the conditioned world.
So why do you argue whether God
is beyond everything or inside everything?

If you see everything and everybody
as your own home,
then neither pleasure nor pain
can permeate the truth of you.

There, Love is always revealed.
There, Love is wrapped in light.
There, light lies on Love's seat
and rests upon Love's crown.

Kabir says, "The True Master is made
completely of light."

HOW CAN IT EVER BE DESCRIBED?

The world is endless, my sister, my brother!
There is only the One that cannot be named,
of whom nothing can be said.

It's not like anything that can be heard or spoken ~
only the soul who actually knows it
has reached that sacred land.

No form, no body, no space is ever present there.
How could I ever begin to tell you
what it actually is?

You come to Love's path only when
God's grace descends,
and then you become free of birth and death.

Kabir says, "It can't be told with words.
It can't be written on paper.
It's like a speechless person who
tastes a very sweet thing ~
how can it ever be described?"

WHY SPEAK OF JUST ONE SUN?

The day has come!
Let us go now to that land where the Beloved lives,
the enchanter of my heart!

There, Love is always filling her vessel
from the endless well,
yet she has no rope with which
to pull up the sweet water.

There are no clouds in the sky there,
yet there are always gentle showers.

O, you boundless One!
Don't sit on your doorstep ~
go outside and play in the rain!
There, it's never dark,
and there's always Moonlight shining.

Why speak of just one Sun?
That country is illuminated with the rays
of billions of Suns.

THE TRUE NAME

The True Name is unlike any other name.
The discrimination between the conditioned
and the unconditioned is meaningless.

The unconditioned is a seed,
the conditioned, flower and fruit.
The branches are knowledge,
but the True Name is the root.

If you look deeply, you will find the root,
and happiness will always be yours.
Then the root will bring you back
to the leaf, the flower, and the fruit.

SHE WILL FILL HER GRANARY

Clouds grow thick in the vast sky ~
listen to the thunder's deep, rumbling voice!
Rain pours in from the East
with its incessant splashing song.

Take good care
with the boundaries of your fields
so the rains don't overflow them.
Prepare your soil with Love,
soaked by the rains of surrender.

Only the wakeful farmer actually
brings her harvest home.
She will fill her granary and feed both
the wise ones and the saints.

THE GAME OF JOY

Kabir reflects and says,
"The One with no lineage or country,
the One with no form or character,
fills the entire Universe."

The Beloved breathed into being
this game of joy ~
from OM all of creation emerged.

The Beloved rejoices in the Earth, the Sky,
the flashing Sun and the silver Moon;
there is joy equally in the beginning,
the middle, and in the end.

There is joy in eyes, in seeing darkness,
and in seeing light.
Joy in the ocean and in the waves ~
in the rivers Sarasvati, Yamuna, and the Ganges.

Love is one: life and death,
union and separation
are all the play of Love's infinite joy.

The Beloved spreads its cover of joy
across the Land, Earth, Sea, Sky, Solar System,
Galaxy ~ across the entire Universe!
Creation is spread out across
the great quilt of Love's joy.

Kabir says, "The whole world resides
in the play of Love,
while the Player remains
hidden and unseen."

WHY NOT GIVE YOURSELF COMPLETELY?

My dear friend, think about this carefully!
If you truly love, then why do you stay asleep?
And if you've already found Love,
why not give yourself completely?
Why do you lose your Beloved
over and over again?

If the peace of deep sleep is already yours,
why waste time making the bed
and rearranging the pillows?

Kabir says, "I'll tell you the truth about Love:
even if you have to cut off
your own head as an offering,
you will do it gladly!"

SO SINGS KABIR

Today is the most treasured of all days!
Today, the Beloved is a guest
in my own home!

Love's presence fills all my rooms,
my courtyard, and my gardens.

I was singing my inner longing
for Love and lost myself
in the Beloved's great beauty.

I wash the Beloved's feet.
I look deeply into Love's eyes.
I lay down my body and mind,
and all that is mine, as an offering.

Today is the most treasured of all days!
My Beloved has come to my house ~
my wealth, my gold, my fulfillment!

All doubt leaves me.
My heart is pure.
My Love has opened my heart to truth.
So sings Kabir,
servant of all servants.

THE SPINNING WHEEL

The woman who is separated from her lover
weaves at the spinning wheel.

The township of the body rises up
with its immaculate beauty,
and inside its walls, a palace for the mind
has been carefully built.

The wheel of Love spirals in the open sky,
and the revolving seat is made of the
precious jewels of wisdom and understanding.

The woman weaves subtle, fine threads
with loving reverence.

Kabir says, "I am weaving the fabric
of night and day.
When my lover comes,
I will lie down at Love's feet,
shedding my tears as an offering."

THE BELOVED LIVES INSIDE

The Beloved lives inside of me
and the Beloved lives inside of you ~
just as the sapling lives inside the seed.
Let go of all pretense and false wanting
and seek for the Beloved within.

A billion blazing Suns shine there,
spreading light across the sea of sky inside.
In this world, I become still and surrender
all notions of blame and wrongdoing.

Dance to the sound of unstruck drums!
Feel Love's exquisite delight!
Feel the rains of no-water
where rivers are streams of light.

One Love permeates the entire Universe,
although very few can see it.

You'll never get home
with your thoughts and your reason!
They are the very cause of all separation.

How blessed is Kabir that, in the midst of all this joy,
he can sing inside his sacred body-vessel.
His music is the sound of one soul
meeting another soul.
It is the melody of remembrance,
where all sorrows are forgotten.
It is the music that transcends
all coming and all going.

SPEAK WHAT IS MOST ALIVE

Hang up Love's swing today,
don't wait any longer!

Hang your body and your mind
between the Beloved's arms,
and swing there in the ecstasy of joy!

Bring the cloud's rainy deluge to your eyes
and cover your heart with the shadow
of the night that fast approaches.

Bring your face all the way up to the Beloved's ear
and speak what is most alive
in your heart.

Kabir says, "Listen friend!
Bring the clearest vision you have of the Beloved
into the very core of your being."

A PLOT OF THISTLE

This world is an insignificant paper parcel ~
even the slightest rain can wash it away.

This world is a plot of thistle,
tangled and trapped in pain.

This world is all kindling and wood,
ready to burn us up as a sacrifice.

Kabir says, "Listen friend,
the True Name of your Beloved
is your lasting homeland
and your ultimate destination."

THE HEAT OF WANTING

The entire world is really
the City-of-Truth ~
its labyrinths thrill the heart.

We can all reach our destination
without ever going anywhere.
This is how Spirit's
unending game is played!

Where songs of abundant joy
dance all around the heart-temple,
there vibrates the play of eternal bliss.

When we truly experience this,
then all gain and loss are extinguished.
From now on, the heat of wanting
can never burn us again!

THE SIGNS OF A MASTER WEAVER

You haven't even begun to figure out
any of the Weaver's real secrets ~
and it only took a moment to spread
the entire Universe out upon Love's loom.

While you were inside listening
to the *Puranas* and the *Vedas*,
I was out here lengthening the threads
for my warp and my weft.

The great Weaver shaped Love's loom
out of Earth and Sky ~
Sun and Moon maneuvered effortlessly
as the Weaver's twin shuttles.

When the great One
worked the levers of the loom together,
I recognized the signs of a Master Weaver
inside my own home.

Kabir says, "I've destroyed my loom;
only the real Weaver can join
separate threads together."

THE CHANCE FOR A HUMAN LIFE

Without the Beloved, joy is fleeting.
The mind is a frenzied elephant,
delirious, and prone to forgetting.

Fire and air may burn as one,
just like the moth,
drawn naturally to the light,
flying feverishly to its death ~
wing and flame burn there together.

Indulging in mindless moments of pleasure,
you forget the truth inside of you
and pursue the lies you hold so close.

You easily forget that old age and death
are never far from you,
although you still indulge in
desire and chase after excitement.

The world is filled with illusions
and false-seeing.
This is just the way of it.
If you have the chance for a human life,
why do you needlessly waste
and destroy it?

HAFIZ

To The One-Love Inside

LIKE A CANDLE BURNING

In my constant love for you,
acclaimed among the luminous ones,
I am like a candle burning.

Sitting at night on life's troubled road
with the broken hearted and the thieves,
I am like a candle burning.

Day and night, I see this strange
worshipping of grief.
I can't sleep, and with this sense
of separation from you,
my tears become a candle burning.

With these clippings of grief for you,
the threads of my patience
become severed.
See what the fire burns away!
All consuming,
I am like a candle burning.

Among both fire and water,
so full of desire for you,
my fragile heart is slowly melting,
like a candle burning.

Within this deep heartache
I become soft, like wax dripping
a mountain of patience at your feet.

Inside the water and fire of love for you,
melting away,
I am like a candle burning.

⸻✦⸻

THE FRIEND'S INTRICATE MYSTERY

⸻✦⸻

I arrive at your door empty handed,
without riches or power.
I've left the path of entering and leaving ~
where is there to go anyway?
And what could I possibly do to arrive?

What journey could possibly matter?
For only in time do I feel
the pain of apparent loss.

But with an open heart
grief found no place in me,
and the bird of separation
had no place to land or perch there.

Hafiz! Be content with Love's pain.
Be silent! The Friend's intricate mystery
can never be seen by reasonable eyes.

⸻✦⸻

LOVE'S TALE HAS NO END

The beauty of Love's tale has no end.
It's an ancient story where words are useless.

There are those who will hurt and disrespect you
with their pride and selfishness.

In your perfect beauty,
you collect hope with the eyes of real seeing.

Hafiz! Walk the path of Love and patience,
for sweet is the cry of lovers!

WHAT WOULD I DO WITHOUT YOU?

Cypress of morning,
with the rose and the rosebud ~
with the braid of the hyacinth,
and the cheek of the lily;
I draw you all close ~
what would I do without you?

Where there is blame, your face is obscured.
So let go of criticism and have compassion
for the dark and angry ones.
This is the sacred work of surrender ~
what would I do without you?

When hidden jealousies ambush you
and strike you like sudden lightning,
do what is necessary and become
a whole harvest consumed ~
what would I do without you?

Shot with the heart-penetrating arrow
of separation, when you shed my blood,
do you say to yourself, "O radiant eye ~
what would I do without you?"

Hafiz! Sublime Paradise is mine
when I'm in the home of my heritage.
In this desolate world, I make my bed
inside the body of you, here and now ~
what would I do without you?

WHERE ALL THINGS ARE REALLY NOTHING

Life is forged in the furnace of this world
where all things are really nothing.

As much as you fill the world's bowl,
there remains only material things and suffering.
There is only one passion that will fulfill
both heart and soul in its search,
and that is the presence of the Beloved.

Love is all that exists.
Without the presence of Love,
heart and soul could never descend
into this troubled world.

An empty cup is the destiny of all:
all must take their fill from life's forceful flood.
Although life's suffering may take you
to the gates of Paradise,
it will not permit you entrance.

Neither the shade of the fruit trees there,
nor the truth of the cypress,
nor the bounty of the garden
will help you if you remain in this world,
where all thing are really nothing.

Your life is short, your hours here
are brief and swift.
So rest awhile before dusk falls,
for time is nothing,
and the sundial's face nothing still.

Linger on the lips of complete surrender,
for short is the distance between
lip and mouth where you journey ~
seize the moment while it's yours,
lift your glass with the Beloved's fill,
for nothing in this world is real.

Think of the rose who always flowers
although she wilts and dies ~
all powers come and go lasting only an hour,
nothing remains of their supremacy.
So don't delude yourself with pride,
you who believed integrity was easy,
and amends given freely.

Between the tavern door and the monastery
lies the great expanse of space
where all things are really nothing.

Like you, I've tasted my salty tears,
and burned in grief's fire ~
why should I cry out to deaf ears?
Suffer silently, for nothing in this world
brings any lasting relief.

Hafiz! You're praised for these songs,
but enduring a tainted or esteemed name,
the lovers of wine will always diminish
your fame in this world,
where all things are really nothing.

UNBEARABLE

Spring breeze, if you can
please send news to my Friend,
with loyalty and devotion, whispering,
"I am consumed in secret and dying!"
Without you, life is unbearable!

NOTHING LEFT TO LOSE
(Written Upon Learning of his Son's Death)

The nightingale sheds drops of his heart's blood
to nourish the red rose ~
but then came a breeze that found
the branches in a jealous mood
and entangled his heart with a hundred thorns.

Just like the parrot nibbling sugar,
this world seemed so sweet and delicious to me,
until the winds of Death
blew all my hopes and dreams away.

Dear light of my eyes,
beloved harvest of my heart,
you will now at least be mine
in precious memory.

So easily you left this world
leaving the most difficult pilgrimage to me!
Camel driver, help me gather the threads
of this fallen load of mine,
and have mercy on me!

The turquoise vault of heaven mixes together
the dust formed on my face,
with the wet tears of my eyes,
and forms the bricks for erecting
this house of joy that is the body.

And still I weep because the Sun,
with shining, jealous glances,
brought on this saddened brow
in lament of my lost Moon,
who found the harbor
of his grave too soon!

SO BRING ME THE CUP AND DRINK

It's unreasonable that I should forsake this wine
in this, the season of the rose.
I speak about reason ~
but this too is unreasonable!

Where is the minstrel?
I can only make the secrets of the harp
and the lyre and the voice of the reed
come alive in the in-breath
of my awareness.

I've become tired of formal learning
and can only serve the Beloved
this perfect wine of the heart.
Loyalty to time leads nowhere ~
so bring me the cup and drink!

I DIE

Inside my desire for your sweet kiss
and your full embrace,
I die.

In the anguish for your glistening,
crimson lips,
I die.

Long is the tale ~ how do I tell it?
I'll make it short:
Come back!
Inside my longing for you,
I die.

THE SHRINE OF THE EYE THAT SEES

When the light of your face
appears to the rose bed of my eye,
my heart rushes to behold you
in the open window of my seeing.

My Beloved, come to me now ~
let your constant arrival
be full of my ruby tears
and the jewels of my heart.

There is a treasure inside the heart.
I'm pulled towards the treasury
of the eye that sees it.

There's no place in this world
that compares to the peace of resting inside
the shrine of the eye that sees.

WHY DO YOU REMAIN SO HIDDEN?

Spring has arrived!
The sweetbriar, the roses, and the tulips
have all pushed their heads up
through the Earth!

And you? Why do you
remain so hidden?

Like Spring's pregnant clouds,
my eyes will shower tears
upon the grave of this imprisoned Earth,
until your precious face pushes
itself up through the soil to meet me!

THE LOVER OF GOD

In my Beloved is my pain and my cure,
a surrendering in my heart and in my life,
also,
to those who profess grace over beauty,
I say to them, "Our Beloved is such a beauty,
one of endless grace,"
also,
the Beloved's smiling face,
the majesty of all worlds ~
to you I've whispered these secrets,
both hidden and seen,
also,
my Friend, in whose veil
we speak these words
that will be told in legends:
our own blood,
which the drunken narcissus shed,
and the Beloved's curls
waving in the breeze,
also,
those endless nights of union,
and the passing away of separation,
and the lover who doesn't fear the judge,
nor the Sultan's punishment,
and calls for more wine,
also,
Hafiz, the lover of God,
the great caretaker
of Suleiman's court.

A SLAVE IN LOVE'S TAVERN

I speak openly, and my words
are happy of heart.
I'm Love's devoted servant in
both form and the formless.

I'm free, flying
like a bird of paradise ~
for what explanation of separation
is even possible now?

What story could I tell of mind's
infinite traps
and how I fell into prison?

I was an angel flying
in the Paradise of Heaven,
until Adam brought me down
into the broken hermitage of this world.

I recognized the star of my Self,
knowing I belonged here on this Earth ~
but under what natal star
was I born?

I've become a slave in Love's tavern:
when a new grief moves in,
I say to it, "Welcome!"

Paint the face of Hafiz with
the ends of your joyous curls,
and my soul will be carried away
in the deluge of this majestic moment.

—◦⦿◦—

IN THE RIVER OF TIME'S SONG

—◦⦿◦—

Everyday, hope for the auspicious sky
to stay put inside
time's ancient turning.

Trembling in the breeze like a willow,
you spoke to me and said,
"Inside the darkness of night
lives all colors."

It was then that my dark hair
turned white
in the river of time's song.

—◦⦿◦—

A FRIEND OF THE SWEET-FACED ONE

I'm a friend of the sweet-faced One,
lost in the tangle of that hair.
I'm troubled with an intoxicated seeing,
with pure wine from old vines.

You ask me, "Can you speak
about the secret of eternity's agreement
that has no beginning?"
I say, "I will tell you the moment
that I drink from the two cups of wine."

Because I'm a lover of God,
I know that there's no escape
from being completely consumed.

I see everything as perfect,
melting into Love's fire ~
I'm a candle that's lost
its fear of the flame.

DRINK IT!

You Wild One,
chanting love songs,
wine cup in hand,
open-hearted and hiding nothing.

With a message in your eyes,
and a love charm on your lips,
you came and sat by my bed
in the Moonlit shade at midnight.

My Love spoke quietly
and in a sad voice said:
"After all these years,
why do you stay asleep?"

The wise access Love's cup ~
fired in the darkness of night
and pressed to honeyed lips.

Whatever portion Love's hand
pours into Life's bowl,
drink it!

SUCH WONDROUS STORIES

I can hear the beating of joy's wings!
I can smell the perfume of my passionate rose!
I can hear the breeze whisper a tale
from Love's lips!
Such wondrous stories I can hear!

YOU HOUSE A GREAT TREASURE

You house a great treasure in your heart,
so why do you regard yourself as poor,
becoming your own worst enemy?

THE END OF ALL SEARCHING

When is news of our union coming?
I will awaken from Earth's green bed
and greet you with open arms!

My soul will be released
from the traps of this world,
and like a hummingbird longing for Paradise,
I will soar to you in freedom, my Love!

When the Beloved's voice
calls me to be a slave,
I transcend both time and mortal life.

So pour down the waters
of your mercy, my Love,
that move me towards eternity.

Bring me wine! Bring me a lute!
Sing so your voice moves through
the folds of my shroud.
I will rise up and dance to your songs.

Arise, and let my eyes
behold your face, my Beloved ~
You: the end of all searching!

WANDERERS ON LOVE'S PATH

We arrive without formality
at the door of the great teacher.
We have come for protection
from the suffering of this world.

We are wanderers on Love's path,
breaking the boundaries of Non-Being,
climbing this ladder of existence
all the way to your gate.

With such treasures as these,
we arrive like beggars,
knocking on your door.

O vessel of divine grace,
you anchor of gentle patience,
in this vast and turbulent
ocean of anguish, we arrive.

Hafiz! Tear off your woolen cloak ~
Love will consume life's great caravan
with the fire of its wailing song.

KEEP YOUR IMAGES TO YOURSELF

Keep your images to yourself ~
nothing can enter this
vision of ours!
Stay on your own side of the street ~
no one else may walk this
path of ours!
Although to most, sleep comes sweetly,
I pray that sleep evades these
eyes of ours!

BECOME THE UNDERSTANDING

Enter my home my Beloved
with your luminosity,
and fill it with the gathering
of perfumed souls.

I have entrusted my heart
to the secret eye of your seeing.

The dust of our gathering
has been stirred up by the breezes
in Love's garden.

Take this incense of you to Paradise
and offer your life up slowly
in the burning of the falling ash.

Become the understanding between
Love's veil and the world's
elusive treasures.

Come shining to the Sun's
brilliant pavilion.

Scatter light from the night's
dark separateness
to the crown of existence,
lighting the lamp of Hafiz like
the full Moon gently rising.

OUT INTO FREEDOM

Messenger of the heart,
bring us news of the Beloved ~
sing us the nightingale's song concerning
the rose's longing to bloom.

For true lovers of friendship,
grief is absent ~
only kindness remains.

Read the message from Love's letter,
and like a beggar, understand
the message it tells.

Love's tresses entangle our hearts,
breaks them to dust, so we may travel
through pain and out into freedom.

If you can pass through this door,
Love's way becomes available to you.

Hafiz! Give me access to this wine,
and let us drink and surrender
all falseness and pretense!

COMPLETELY CLEAR

If you're really seeking the face of the Beloved,
make the mirror of your heart
completely clear!

FROM THE FOUNTAIN OF YOUR RUBY LIPS

Beloved! You are
always bringing me back home.
Without you, there's no air to breathe.
Now, there's no more fear of death
since I drank from the perfumed waters
pouring forth from the fountain
of your ruby lips.

FOR TWO BARLEYCORNS

I see the new crescent Moon
in the green stretch of sky,
and reflect on my own harvested fields
and seasons of sowing and reaping.

Go towards that sky, pure and free,
and you will reach the Sun
in all its magnificence!

Don't rely on the thief of night
to illuminate the heavens ~
he is a fraud, and only reflects.

Tell the sky: "Let go of all vanity;
in the marketplace of Love,
they sell the moon's harvest
for one barleycorn,
and the expanse of the Pleiades
for two barleycorns."

SOON ENOUGH

Don't ever remove your lips
from the lip of Love's cup ~
so the desires of this world
may never keep you separate
from the One-Taste of this wine.

Since the world offers you
both the bitter and the sweet,
desire only the sweet from
the Beloved's lips ~
the bitter from the cup of the world
will come soon enough.

THE VERY DUST OF THIS BODY

The very dust of this body
veils the face of the Beloved.
When I finally drop the veil,
joy's swelling ocean comes rushing in.

The prison of this world
isn't fit for a minstrel like me.
I'm headed for the roses of Ridvan,
where the angel of Paradise is waiting
for this bird of the grassy plains.

It's not clear why I've entered this world,
this place of regret and sorrow,
careless, with my own work to do.

In the infinity of this holy place,
where can I connect with the Universal Mind,
when confined to this, the dust of my body?

ALLOW WINE TO SPILL

My Beloved, please bring me the cup,
and fill it up from your wine,
let me pass it around!

Love seems so easy in the beginning,
but just wait ~ sit and sip awhile!

The Beloved's curls stir up morning's perfume
in the mystery of her braids ~
inside this sweet thicket,
your heart may finally open and break!

There is no real security in
life's travelling guesthouse.
At any moment the bell may sound
and the bindings in your heart may tighten.

So allow wine to spill on your prayer mat
if the tavern's proprietor so desires!
This pull to the things of the world
can only bring you heartache.

Witness the evolution of your soul
from control to surrender ~
you walk that path of mystery
where before all was festivity.

A mountain of waves pound and roar;
the dark sky becomes clouded over ~
how can anyone really know the journey
to reach that other shore?

Hafiz! Always abide in Love,
and Love will always be!
One glance from this adored face,
and be lost to time and space.

NO WORTH

If there is sorrow,
the delight of existence
has no worth.

If there is cruelty,
all the fortunes in the world
have no worth.

If there are just five days of heartache,
seven thousand years of joy
have no worth.

GOOD ADVICE

Beloved rose of exquisite beauty,
you sit all day with the thorns ~
they must give you good advice!

From your gardens, a breeze of desire blows ~
for your fragrance saturates everything here,
like the wild roses dancing in the wind.

You are drawing me towards you
like the delicate candle burning ~
you are more worthy than
Jalal ad-Din Rumi's banquet halls!

Let my heart endure the deluge
of these flowing tears ~
let my eyes save me
so I may finally see
what is real!

COME WITH ME MY BELOVED!

Come with me my Beloved!
This wine is the soul-treasure of life
fit only for a broken heart.

Give yourself completely ~
pitch your life like a tent across the world
and your canopy will reach into the heavens!

Come with me my Beloved!
Your blazing cup is the sparkling Sun
and the silver Moon.

Give yourself completely,
and I'll spread my whole court
across the great expanse of such a sky!

Come with me my Beloved!
This wine of ours is eternal.

Bring the cup to your lips
and become intoxicated forever!
With such pure wine inside me,
I will sing you songs that always please.

Come with me my Beloved!
Your adoring gaze is like
a banquet hall in Paradise,
full of sweet perfume and gentle light.

So take this cup, don't fear ~
inside it flows only happiness.
In this garden of Paradise,
this wine is wise medicine.

THE BELOVED IS HERE!

I kiss the Beloved's lips.
I drink the Beloved's wine.
I dance in the sacred waters of life.

How could I ever begin to tell you
the depth of this mystery?
How could I ever compare anything
or anyone to the Beloved's face?

In this cup, you can drink
the Beloved's ruby lips
and the blood that flows within.

Like the intoxicated eyes of the Beloved,
offer wine to the memory of
those crimson lips.

The soul doesn't seek separation
from the body ~
the blood of the cup runs
in the body's veins!

The rose has returned to the garden
and has brought along its throne ~
like the folded rose bud,
make your prayer rug exact and exalted.

O Minstrel of the Moon,
play your harp, hand extended,
with grace and beauty so that I may rejoice!

When the morning owl wails:
"The Beloved is here!"
don't put down your cup,
"The Beloved is here!"
Drink with the Sultan of the rose
and be happy!
Gain the freedom of the
stars and seasons.

Hafiz! Be silent!
Listen to the unspoken truth
spoken by the tongueless reed.

—⟨∞⟩—

THAT YOU KNOW SO WELL

I'm searching for a trace of the
morning breeze of happiness
that you know so well!

On a certain street,
I pass at a certain time,
that you know so well!

You are the gatekeeper
at the chamber of mystery ~
I keep my eyes on the destination
of that path,
that you know so well!

O Beloved, I write only a few words
in such a way
that no stranger could understand ~
but by your kindness,
you read them with infinite recognition,
that you know so well!

Hafiz! It doesn't matter
what language you speak ~
Love's telling describes it in every language,
that you know so well!

YOUR OWN SUFFERING

Don't give your heart to the world
and its shiny objects.
You'll never experience
true fidelity there.

In the world, sweet honey comes
with a sting,
luscious dates with bitter thorns.
No one's kindled lamp is ever spared
being blown out by time's wind.

Look, and you will see:
when you give your heart to the world,
you begin to treasure your own suffering.

NO CLUE

The wise doctor has no clue
the remedy for my pain.
Without the Friend,
my heart is shattered.
With the Friend,
eternal happiness is mine!

WILD ONES ARE WE

If you become like me,
caught in the Beloved's glorious snare,
drunk on wine and the cup
you will be!

Intoxicated, annihilated,
wild ones are we!
Don't sit with us if you care
about name or form or reputation.

SEEK SUCH A WOUND

Sit with the Friend ~
seek the wine of Love's cup.
From the lips of the cypress comes
the sought after kiss.

When the ease of the wound rises,
the point of Love's piercing eases.
Seek such a wound
with gratitude!

TO THE ONE-LOVE INSIDE

Most live their lives identified to ego,
prideful and asleep.
For them union is always denied.

You must relinquish your reason
and your knowing
and visit the tavern of the wild,
raving lovers!

What do you know of that
drunken madness?
What doors will those Earthly
juices open?

Fall in love with the Moon
and open your heart to the truth,
though you still believe
you are somebody.

Tell everything that's locked
inside your secret heart
to the One-Love inside
who's listening.

Let the cup of wine clear your mind Hafiz!
Drink deeply so you may finally
forget yourself!

BIOGRAPHICAL NOTES

RUMI (1207-1273)

Rumi was born into a prestigious family of scholars in Balkh (present-day Afghanistan), and later settled in Konya, Anatolia (present-day Turkey). Like his father, he was a highly respected teacher, jurist, and theologian. In 1244, Rumi met the wandering dervish Shams of Tabriz who turned his world upside down, opened his spiritual heart, and set fire to his life. The two spent nearly four years together in a sublime and ecstatic state of almost inseparable union. After the disappearance of Shams (some say murdered by jealous students), Rumi began his prolific outpouring of nearly 70,000 verses in both the Divan-e Shams-e Tabrizi, and the Mathnawi, which have graced the world with their profound wisdom and beauty for nearly 750 years.

KABIR (C. 1440-1518)

Kabir was born into a family of Muslim weavers in Varanasi, India. At an early age, he became a student of the great Hindu teacher Ramananda, a leader in the Bhakti movement of 14th century northern India. Kabir was deeply critical of both Muslim and Hindu traditions, embracing his teacher's monist Advaitist belief that there is but one single source of reality and that this source lives inside of us. Kabir was a householder with a wife and children. He became a master weaver, revered teacher, and a mystical poet of great fame with a diverse following of students from all religions and traditions. His poems are wonderfully humorous and tender in their criticism of the traditional rituals and customs of his day. His poems consistently point to the reality that God lives within each of us and must always be sought for, and found, within.

HAFIZ (C. 1320-1389)

Hafiz was born and lived in the beautiful garden city of Shiraz, Persia (present-day Iran). He was renowned throughout the Islamic world as a master lyrical genius, and gained widespread fame and recognition in his own lifetime. It is presumed he had a wife and children and became an Islamic scholar and teacher, gaining the support of wealthy patrons, and eventually teaching religious studies at a university in Shiraz. He began studying with the great Sufi master Muhammad Attar as a young man, and studied almost daily with him until he reached his enlightenment just after his sixtieth birthday. His collected works (The Divan) are a classic of Sufi literature, revered throughout the Islamic world, as well as by Emerson and Goethe in the West. For centuries, Hafiz has been referred to as *The Tongue of the Invisible* for his unique ability to express the inexpressible and convey a taste of the divine love and union present in the awakened heart.

SELECT BIBLIOGRAPHY

RUMI

Arberry, A.J. *Mystical Poems of Rumi, Volumes 1&2* (poems 1-400).
Chicago: University of Chicago Press, 2009.

Nicholson, R.A. *The Mathnawi of Jalalu'ddin Rumi, 6 vols.*
Konya: Konya Metropolitan Municipality, 2008.

_____. *Selected Poems from the Divan-e Shams-e Tabrizi.*
Bethesda: Ibex Publishers, 2001.

Thackston, Jr. W.M. *Signs of the Unseen: The Discourses of Jalaluddin Rumi.*
Putney: Threshold Books, 1994.

KABIR

Dharwadker, Vinay. *Kabir: The Weaver's Songs.*
New Delhi: Penguin Books India, 2003.

Sethi, V.K. *Kabir: The Weaver of God's Name.*
New Delhi: Radha Soami Satsang Beas, 1984.

Tagore, Rabindranath. *Songs of Kabir.*
Boston: Red Wheel/Weiser Books. 2002.

HAFIZ

Arberry, A.J. *Hafiz: Fifty Poems.*
Cambridge: Cambridge University Press. 1953.

Bell, Gertrude. *The Garden of Heaven: Poems of Hafiz.*
Mineola: Dover Thrift Editions. 2003

Clarke, H. Wilberforce. *The Divan-I-Hafiz.*
Bethesda: Ibex Publishers, 2007.

CPSIA information can be obtained
at www.ICGtesting.com
Printed in the USA
BVOW09s1000150318

510671BV00015B/319/P